Touch the Whale

Overcome Fears and Self-limitations

Live Your Life to the Fullest

Heidi Cowie

Manor House

Touch the Whale

Library and Archives Canada Cataloguing in Publication

Cowie, Heidi, 1955-
 Touch the whale : overcome fears and self-limitations, live your life to the fullest / Heidi Cowie.

ISBN 978-1-897453-35-3

 1. Self-actualization (Psychology). 2. Self-confidence. I. Title.

BF637.S4C685 2012   158.1   C2012-907727-5

Published 2012: Manor House Publishing Inc., 452 Cottingham Crescent, Ancaster, ON, CANADA, L9G 3V6 905-648-2193 wwww.manor-house.biz

All rights reserved

Cover Design: Donovan Davie / Michael Davie   Cover photo: TsuneoMP/Shutterstock

 We acknowledge the financial support of the Government of Canada through the Canada Book Fund (CBF) for our publishing activities.

I would like to thank my husband and daughter for their unwavering support, love, acceptance, and being my cheerleaders.

To my best friend Priya Ali who carved out space in her home and life every Monday morning so we feed off each other's energy and creativity.

Thanks to my publisher Michael Davie of Manor House for his belief in my project.

About Touch the Whale:

Join stress management expert **Heidi Cowie** as she shines a glowing light on the bumpy path to a brilliant and fearless life in her newest release, *Touch the Whale*. The book is an inspiring and often hilarious collection of stories about the adventures and mishaps that helped Heidi become more courageous and resilient. Her gentle lessons and ironic insights are delivered with compassion, honesty and the sure knowledge that change is possible for each of us.

Each chapter contains exercises and meditations to help readers extend their "safety zones" while dissolving stress-inducing beliefs; the book is guaranteed to help readers develop attitudes that create more happiness, achieve greater success and control the annoying "little voice" that prevents dreams from becoming realities.

Foreword

Touch the Whale is a graceful adventure into the many aspects of embracing uncertainty while letting go of fear.

In a series of witty and at times harrowing vignettes, the book traces author Heidi Cowie's growing understanding of how her fears had been holding her back from living the abundant and joyful life she desired.

Step by riveting step, Cowie describes how she was able to release her worries and begin embracing uncertainty in the story of an evolution that has had dramatic benefits.

Yes, Cowie actually did touch a whale, in the wild, in the ocean. She also swung from a trapeze from a dizzying height – and she's frequently stepped well outside her comfort zone to embrace uncertainty and grow from each experience.

The book also includes a series of practical exercises designed to help the reader follow Cowie on the unpredictable path to peace of mind.

Cowie's writing style is lively and refreshing; her wisdom is timeless and entertaining. An irresistible read!"

Susan Crossman, author, *Passages to Epiphany* and *Shades of Teale*

Touch the Whale

"Thinking about it now, I am certain that had I known what could happen out there on the ocean, I never would have gone... I saw a whale swimming and all I heard was a whooshing sound as the whale breeched the surface... As the next one breeched, I reached my hand out to touch it and at that point, I knew my life would be different. When I reached out, I felt disconnected from my body, feeling as if I didn't own my arm and that it was moving out on it's own volition. When I felt the whale, this electricity ran throughout my body, there was absolutely no fear, and an overwhelming feeling of being blessed..."

- Heidi Cowie

Chapter 1 — Touch the Whale

When I tell people I have touched a whale they look at me as if I just discovered a cure for cancer. It really wasn't *that* big of a deal. I mean, touching the whale was a life altering moment for sure, but actually wandering into the neighbourhood of whales? Now that's actually the story that begs to be told.

The woman who had initially presented me with the invitation to go kayaking with whales was a friend who turned out to have a fear of water. Who knew? It was a bit surprising since she was a psychologist and I had assumed – incorrectly – that she was every bit as confident and competent in the water as she was at an ink blot convention.

At the time, I was working full-time as a pharmaceutical manager and attending university on a part time basis. Well, I was actually clocking *full-time* hours at school and basically all I did was work and study. Any time away from my job was taken up by studying and writing so when my friend called, it really was an opportunity to have some good old fun. And boy, was I ready to have fun!

I suppose in the middle of February, any diversion would seem tasty but my friend's offer of a seven-day kayak trip around the coast of Cape Breton Island had the tang of adventure that was utterly lacking in my school library. Thinking for a quick minute that I would be in the North Atlantic – the Ocean! – I decided it was a great idea! Have I mentioned yet that I had never been in a kayak? And of course, nowhere in any of our pre-adventure discussions did my friend reveal the fact that she was likely to be so paralyzed by her fear of water that she would be completely incapable of actually *paddling* a kayak. Little did I know before we set out that the first 20 minutes would prove to be eye-openers. I loved a good challenge. But then the trouble was destined to begin.

In retrospect, I realize that we didn't really think this trip out at all well. I went to an outfitter store in Waterloo, which was part of my sales territory at the time, and when I told the sales clerk what I would be doing, he shuddered and made me buy very expensive outdoor clothing. The sales clerk had been born and raised in Cape Breton and he knew the unpredictability and viciousness of the weather. Thankfully, he never shared that with me and just ensured I had all the gear I needed to keep me dry.

As I was trying on the clothes, I shared the itinerary with the shop owner. I explained to him that the one glitch was getting from the Sydney Nova Scotia airport to Chetticamp on Cape Breton Island. There were no buses or trains and renting a car was silly. What came next was just the first taste of the wonderful Cape Bretoners. He got on the phone and called his son who lived in Sydney to ask him to drive us to Chetticamp. I couldn't believe it! His son was delighted to help out.

After the outfitters, I turned my attention to my luggage. At the time I was somewhat younger and less travelled than I am now and I was oblivious to the fact that a suitcase full of clothes is not entirely suitable for a week-long adventure in a kayak. And why *wouldn't* a gal need three pairs of shoes for such a journey?? We landed safely in Sydney and were picked up by Ron and Sheila and driven to Chetticamp.

In due course my friend and I arrived at the lagoon from whence we would depart and we marveled as we saw the boats all lined up as pretty as a row of Smarties. It was beautiful!

We were going with a group of other like-minded adventurers and the excitement of it all had me tingling in anticipation. Until I saw where my clothes were supposed to go. Were they serious? Everything we were going to take with us had to be packed into the holds of those pretty little boats. All the food, plates, cutlery, sleeping bags, boat covers and clothes that 13 people needed for a week on the salty brine, *all of it* had to be stuffed into a handful of boats that had a combined storage area about the size of a desk drawer. I'm kidding. Make that two desk drawers. And where exactly were our legs supposed to go? The suitcases were history. I became acutely aware of how tightly you could actually roll clothes, the motivation being the three pairs of shoes I just couldn't bear to leave behind on the shore.

We finally got everything packed and had a bite to eat: the adventure of a lifetime was about to begin! We stepped gingerly into our kayaks, giddy and petrified. The head guide picked up a paddle and said:

"This is how you go left; this is how you go right; follow the guides and let's go!"

That, folks, was the extent of the instruction.

Thinking about it now, I am certain that had I known what could happen out there on the ocean, I never would have gone. Thankfully, at the beginning of the voyage, I was blissfully ignorant. What I was sure about was that my boat would never roll right over. When I was a kid, I had nearly drowned in the undertow at Ontario's Long Point Beach, so I had a fear of water. Well, actually I was afraid of dying in the water. The water itself was probably OK. But I was confident those days were behind me now, everything was going to be just fine.

Our guides were lovely (*very* lovely, especially the cute one I nicknamed Sweater Boy) and eventually they realized I could not single-handedly chauffeur the fear-paralyzed woman in my kayak for the full trip.

How elated I was the next day when another good-looking and incredibly virile young guide took the front seat of the kayak and pointed me in the direction of one he said was for me alone. The good news/bad news was that I ended up in a single kayak by myself and experienced a freedom that was similar in scope to what I felt after divorcing my first husband. Picture my glee as the wind and the sea wafted across my delicate features.

Perhaps not *too* delicate.

Now all anyone had to figure out was where one was supposed to dispose of cigarette filters. You got it. I smoked and I don't mind telling you that arranging my life around this habit was quite the experience. I would smoke while paddling, which made the others laugh and I could never bring myself to throw the butts into the ocean. The darned things don't disintegrate so I had a vision of me personally polluting all the Earth's precious seas. It was cringe-worthy. So the only thing I could think of to do was to put my butts under the springy ropes on the top of the boat. They looked like little soldiers all lined up in a row. But I'm getting ahead of myself. Let's get back to the whales.

I really give credit to the guides because I do think they had eyes sprouting out of all parts of their heads. They generally kept us close in to shore (remember this was my first time in a kayak).

On Day Two of the trip they spotted a pod of whales off in the distance. The guides gave us an option. We could paddle out to the pod or watch from the shore. We all started paddling. As I started to paddle out, I was mesmerized by the calm waters around the kayak and the spray from the whales in the distance. I was on that precipice where I desperately wanted to be near a whale and yet, terrified as well. It was really a double whammy because this was the first time we paddled far off shore and no one really knew what to expect when we got closer to the pod. The guides told us the whales were called pilot whales and were no bigger than dolphins. They lied. These whales were huge but we would never know it from their behaviour. The guides corralled some of us into a circle and then each adventurer hung on to their neighbours' boats. I was comfortable not hanging on to the next boat so I drifted away from the circle a bit. Some of the other kayakers did the same and no one was saying a word. We trusted that the guides had seen and experienced this before. And then I looked at one of them and he looked scared.

At that point, I questioned my decision, took a deep breath, concentrated on paddling and moved in closer to where I last saw a whale. I knew that I would likely not have this opportunity again and believed that we needed to take the magnificent moments when they are put in front of us. I could feel the sweat trickle down my back despite the cool breeze. My throat felt constricted and I was unable to talk. I could feel my legs shaking as my feet were steering the rudder. I kept going because deep inside, I knew I would be O.K.

It was quiet.

In the gap between young virile Sweater Boy and myself, I saw a whale swimming and all I heard was a whooshing sound as the whale breeched the surface. We could hear the whales chatter to each other under water. When I heard their music, I instantly became calm- I had never heard anything quite as beautiful. They were gentle and respectful of our space and our fear. As the next one breeched, I reached my hand out to touch it and at that point, I knew my life would be different. When I reached out, I felt disconnected from my body, feeling as if I didn't own my arm and that it was moving out on it's own volition. When I felt the whale, this electricity ran throughout my body, there was absolutely no fear, and an overwhelming feeling of being blessed.

My life since then has been different.

For years ever after, I would tell this story and feel the thrill sear through my body as if I were still there with the whales. I've shared this story with many people in the hope that they too could be transformed, even for just one brief moment of pure innocence and glory.

The rest of the trip was a bit anti-climactic. We got used to the whales and the sound of waves on our beach as we slept onshore at night. We would drop into bed, exhausted from the effort of paddling all day and then having to haul boats full of seven days' worth of food and equipment out onto the shore every evening.

After a day of kayaking, my friend would stand by the fire with her Tilley hat on and her arms crossed over her chest and just watch everyone hauling the boats, gathering the food, and helping with the meals and the cleaning. And she just stood there. Annoying? You bet!

The entire troop was irritated by her behaviour but nothing was said. Finally, on the last day, I asked her why she hadn't contributed and she told me she had paid to be on *vacation*. Of course! How stupid of me. And I guess it was my job to look after her? Ugh.

In any event the last day was miserable, the only day out of the seven where the weather had not been lovely. That's quite normal for the Cape Breton coast, apparently. The weather there can be fickle and we were told that kayakers had often had to hike out of the wilderness because the wind was too fierce to allow anyone to make headway in a small boat.

That last day saw us paddling into a lagoon that had a fresh water waterfall cascading down into it. We each took a turn bathing in the frigid water and screaming at the cold. But we were ever so grateful to feel clean again!

We noticed the wind began to pick up around midday and it continued to increase in intensity throughout the afternoon. The guides made the decision to stay put until sunset, since the winds usually lessen around that time of day.

As I mentioned, being a smoker at the time was a source of entertainment for some of the group. I must have been quite a sight — picture a pretty lady paddling a kayak with a cigarette dangling out the side of her mouth.

Nice image, right?

Naturally, there were only a limited number of cigarettes left by the last day of the trip and any other smokers in the group had run out by then as well. If you've ever been a smoker, you can imagine my sadness as I finally extinguished my very last cigarette and placed it fondly with the other dead soldiers under the rope of my kayak. This was not good! Picturesque as this all was, many of us needed a smoke and we finally hit upon the brilliant idea of rolling grass (I'm talking about sod here) into papers someone had brought along for an entirely different type of smoke. We had a good giggle at our ingenuity and it all lightened the bit of anxiety that we were all feeling at the thought of having to paddle, beach, unpack and repack in the dark.

The night paddle was incredible. The guides had a system whereby each paddler was assigned a number and we would call the numbers out one by one so no-one would get lost. The remarkable part of the experience was the phosphorescence that would come up on the paddles each time they were lifted out of the water. It looked like sparkling strands of angel hair in all different colours. It was mesmerizing!

We eventually reached our destination, John Cabot Beach, in safety. We managed to haul all the boats up this incredibly huge hill, and unpack and repack the waiting cars for our drive back to our starting point of Chetticamp.

A year later I returned to the beach and chuckled at what I thought was a "huge" hill. It was, in reality, nothing more than a big step up but I guess when we had been hauling boats full of gear at midnight, it had felt huge.

I reflect upon my friend from time to time and think of how much I admire her. Despite the fact that she was perceived as a little on the lazy side, she achieved a huge milestone on that trip that had nothing to do with touching a giant whale. Her "whale" was her fear of water and on the very last day of the trip she came to the realization that she had left it behind her. She was no longer afraid. Of course everybody was ready to kill her by then. But we all have reasons for doing what we do, often without even knowing why.

Besides learning about courage, the trip taught me that the feelings of peace and connectedness to nature and others is essential to our emotional wealth and health. I was profoundly affected by the sounds of the water and the gentle slicing of my paddle as I maneuvered along rugged coastlines. It comforted me to leave the wildlife undisturbed.

After the trip, I bought my own kayak. She was a flaming red, Boreal carbon-Kevlar sea kayak. I loved spending the weekends paddling in different bodies of water and experimenting with her in different waves and winds.

My boat brought me to areas of this province of Ontario that I never would have seen: Georgian Bay, the shores of Lake Huron (Port Elgin, Southampton), the shores of Lake Erie, beaches along Lake Ontario (Port Dalhousie and the Binbrook Conservation area!) She even brought me down to Nova Scotia where I spent my summer vacation for three years in a row.

I rented a fabulous house on the footsteps of the bay that led to Cherry Hill beach. The house was in a tiny village named Vogler's Cove, population 300. I was quite the ticket for the townsfolk. They all thought I was off my rocker paddling a kayak.

"These waters are meant for proper fishing boats," they'd tell me. I didn't care. I travelled from one end of the province to another. I saw the tide come in on the

Bay of Fundy, I travelled to Annapolis Valley and all the way back to Chetticamp on Cape Breton Island.

Every time I sat in my boat I was overwhelmed with a feeling of pride, accomplishment, and adventure. My spirit was glowing and during the paddle I felt connected, as if all the systems in my body were humming with the universal rhythms of nature and man.

So what's the lesson in all this?

Lesson #1: Marvel at the Wonder

The lesson is, marvel at the wonder. Marvel at the wonder of a woman's resiliency, bravery, and courage in putting herself in the most terrifying situation possible so she could conquer her worst fear. My friend symbolized for me the height of courage. She decided to be purposeful in conquering her fears and really didn't give a hoot what anyone else thought. That was also a huge example for me. How many of us stop being or doing what we want, or being who we are because of the fear of what others might think?

That's about Judgment. It can paralyze us and destroy our true spirits of joy, bliss, self awareness.

I invite you also to marvel at the ability to share space with wild creatures while respecting their place in life. Marvel at the ability to get used to the extraordinary beauty and ugliness of life. Marvel at the beauty of complete silence outside and inside your brain.

I think when we are in the presence of natural magnificence, it humbles us with regards to our limitations. At times, being in the Cape Breton environment allowed me to really hear for the first time. I remember lying in my sleeping bag and asking the ocean waves to be quieter. Yet I loved every minute of their roaring!

Being that close to nature and truly living with Her made me realize how disconnected I had become from nature in my "normal" life. The sounds of cell phones, traffic, TVs and all the other modern noises that are part of our lives seemed to be so loud upon my return to my life!

I had become so entrenched in my busyness that I became detached from what I was actually feeling and being. I wondered to myself, if it was so easy to disconnect from my spirit and sense of being, then how easy is it to disconnect and detach from others? This lack of connectedness affects all our systems — mental, emotional, physical, and spiritual.

This trip taught me that "being" requires vigilance. A checking in, if you will, on a daily basis to make sure you are on track and can still connect the dots. Today, whenever I am able, I ground myself with a walk in a forest or a park. I believe that being in nature truly does ground us to Mother Earth, the origin of all mankind.

I hug trees — there I've said it for the world to know! I imagine that the strength and the life force in the tree is being transmitted into my body. I feel the energy from my body being rooted and I visualize the roots being as strong and far reaching as the tree. It's a terrific grounding experience if you don't mind the odd stare. When I am unable to get to the park and am in a tough situation, I visualize the tree in my mind's eye and I feel the energy shifting.

"There is only that moment, and the incredible certainty that everything under the sun has been written by one hand only."— Paulo Coelho

Marvel at the Wonder Reflections

Take some time right now and start writing without editing yourself. Allow your thoughts to flow freely as you think of these questions:

What adventure do you dream of completing?

What prevents you from following this dream?

What is your worst fear?

What fears do you need to eliminate?

What do you need to embrace?

How do you connect to your spirit?

What can you do to replenish your energy?

Chapter 2 — Men in Tights

I had the good fortune to work for a pharmaceutical company for 15 years and part of the joy of the experience was that the annual national sales meetings almost always occurred off shore.

Once we went to the Dominican Republic. The tourism industry was just getting started there and we had to gather for our first company meeting in the space where all the evening entertainment took place.

The resort was clearly not set up for our sales meeting. There we were, sitting around a table that was entirely open to the rest of the resort. We were expected to listen to a boring presentation on profit margins while the surging surf beckoned and beautiful people walked by us in their bikinis!

Eventually the distractions were too much for us and staff from the resort hung bedspreads around us so we couldn't see out. It was like a prison in Paradise!

The next year, my company sales meeting took place at a Club Med in Florida (good decision folks!) and the resort featured a circus school. After a few days of walking by the trapeze, I decided to climb the sucker and give it a shot.

One of my colleagues was from Vancouver and she had spent years dancing ballet. Lilly was a tiny woman, probably a size two, and she had teeny size five feet that looked even smaller when compared to my generous size 10s!

Where the difference really mattered to me was on the ladder leading up to the trapeze: the rungs were only about a foot long so maneuvering my two feet gracefully upwards was a bit tricky.

Lilly climbed the ladder effortlessly ahead of me and the grace and elegance of a ballerina infused her every movement; once at the top she grabbed the bar and flew through the air as if she had been doing it forever.

Then it was my turn. The ladder went straight up to the platform and it swung a bit as I stepped onto each rung. My natural inclination was to look down, which was only terrifying because I had a fear of heights!

The instructor kept shouting, "don't look down!" What did he know? Our brains don't know what "don't," "not," and "no" mean — in fact, the brain translates those words into "do," "yes," and "yes!" If I tell you, "don't think of a pink umbrella," you are going to think of a pink umbrella. Just a tip for you parents out there: stop using the word "don't" on your kids because their brains are actually hearing "DO!"

I never really gave too much thought to the trapeze`s height before I stood at the top of the ladder; I sure came face to face to reality when I started to see the rooftops of the resort buildings. They were a long way down. Or maybe I was a long way up! It had seemed to take me forever to get to the top but there I was. Frozen atop this ladder and expected to step out onto a platform about the size of two floor tiles. On the other side of a great canyon of space stood the instructor. He kept sending the trapeze across to me through the air (not with the greatest of ease, I might add).

Apparently, "all I had to do" was grab the bar and step off the little platform and into the void. Simple right? Right. That's probably why at least a dozen times I had to ask, "So you want me just to step off?" I got a resounding "Yes!" each time, after which I decided that it was an insane idea and there was no way on Earth in my lifetime that I would grab a bar and just step off.

The next time I would feel this paralyzed would be at the top of a church aisle when I was marrying my second husband. Didn't want to do that so much either! The power of intuition. (I'm a big believer in trusting your gut!)

I always had the option of climbing back down off the ladder and just forgetting the whole miserable idea but there was a crowd below me cheering me on. How could I disappoint my fans?

Eventually the instructor realized stronger measures were called for. Along came Tactic Number Two. It was magic. This time, as the bar was being thrown over to me, there was a gorgeous man, a Spanish God in skin-tight leopard tights hooked onto it by the knees. His arms were stretched out towards me. Now they wanted me to grab his arms as I stepped off.

Oh my! When was I ever going to get the chance to swing across the sky with a sexy man in tights?

Voilà, done! That bar and that man swung towards me and I grabbed his arms and stepped off. What a ride! I was laughing and squealing the entire time. The crowd below was clapping and cheering, and for a brief moment, it felt as if I could fly. Freedom.

Lesson #2: Just Step Off

Just step off! Fear paralyzes us into non-action. Many times clients complain that they feel stuck as if they cannot move forward but in fact, they are **choosing** not to move forward. At every junction of our lives and all day every day, we have choices. Choice in what we wear, eat, do, and most importantly, choice in how we feel and think.

Our mind is not some inert mass of mush. Our mind is a vital and energetic creator of our reality. Our mind is not our master, but when we are stuck in fear, anxiety, and lack and scarcity, the mind becomes our ruler. We buy into the negative thought patterns and they then become our reality.

For the most part, this is how our brains physically function: neurons that fire together wire together. The more we think a thought, the faster it manifests in our lives. As I was thinking of the trapeze and climbing the ladder, the thought was "this is very scary" and that thought created many physical responses. My heart rate and blood pressure increased, cortisol began shooting through my blood stream, and all my organs were in high alert. Our mind creates a response in our bodies so think about this: if you constantly fear illness, lack and abandonment, what do you think your body is creating in response to these thoughts?

Negative thoughts and beliefs produce a negative physical reaction. There is ample research on the body, mind, and spirit connection to prove this point.

Often, what I hear as a therapist is that the negative thoughts are reality and the positive thoughts are just wishes. I had one client who thought negatively about each contract he bid on so when he didn't get it, he wouldn't be disappointed. How many contracts do you think he signed? Never as many as he wanted.

Your thoughts are created by choice. Really— Just step off. Do you really in your heart understand that you have a choice? Not in your head — nice try — in your heart!

Get in touch with that lovely organ that just keeps beating with no requests or prompting from you. It is so wise. The heart knows. Period. We are always trying to intellectualize everything and when did we stray so far from the heart??? Most of us tend to think the mind is right and in control and I am here to tell you that if you give your mind the power to control negatively you are sunk — Titanic style.

Give your mind the control to think positively — then you have a hole in one — a double win! Unless you connect with your heart, your mind will play tricks on you. Your heart never lies because that is where your intuition lives.

According to the Institute of Heartmath, the heart is more intuitive than the brain. The heart receives intuitive information about one second before the brain. In addition, the electromagnetic signals that are sent from the heart are 60 times greater than what is produced by the brain and the signals can be measured in the brain waves of people around us.

Just Step Off Reflections

Take some time right now and start writing without editing yourself. Allow your thoughts to flow freely as you think of these questions:

How often to you act on your intuition?

How do you let past mistakes influence your current happiness?

Guilt causes many people to do things they do not want to do. How does guilt affect your actions and/or decisions?

What is preventing you from just stepping off into a more joyful life?

In what area of your life do you feel you have no choice?

Chapter 3 — Return to Learn

When I was 42, I decided to return to university. Obviously there was a little more to the decision than waking up one morning with a yen to carry heavy books around with me all day. A lot more, actually.

I was blessed to be working for an amazing pharmaceutical company that was headquartered in Montreal. All the field managers and representatives worked from home and basically managed their own time and territories with no-one breathing down their backs. Because of this freedom, I was able to do other things throughout the day, things that wouldn't be possible in a 9-5 job.

I was also a single mother and my daughter was getting ready to leave for the University of Western Ontario. I was panicking a little because I had invested so much of my time and energy in raising Alexis that I felt that many of my roles in life had suddenly become less critical. I know you never stop mothering, but when the kids are out of the house, it means a whole lot of empty time.

I needed to find a way to bring new meaning into my own life, to fill the spaces left by my shrinking duties as a mother. It didn't take me long to decide that it would be a great idea for me to return to university to complete the BA that I had abandoned back in the mid 70's. I only needed two more courses to complete my degree so why not?

At the same time, I felt pulled to do some volunteer work. I realized that my life was blessed. I had a home, a great job, a healthy daughter…it was all good and I felt that it was time to give back to my community.

I looked around at many agencies and then found a Peer Counsellor role for the Women's Centre at the YWCA. It was a great program that gave women in the community quality counselling by a peer for no charge.

The program didn't accept everyone who wanted to volunteer. I first had to submit a short essay on why I wanted to do this and why I thought I would be good a counsellor.

I was ultimately accepted into the program and I gratefully began my training sessions. That was quite a ride! It meant a great deal of soul searching and self-examination and helping other volunteers to wade through their "garbage." Always more lessons! In due course, I was ready for clients and although I had not yet started my university work, the idea was still bubbling away on a back burner.

The first client I spoke to as a peer counsellor was a beautiful young woman who had had a troubled past. The minute I sat down and began to hear her story, I knew that this was what I wanted to do for the rest of my life. It blew my fan! Every cell in my body felt tingly and alive, as if I had been in a long sleep and had suddenly awoken to a bright new day. I was so excited and pumped up that I knew this was the right choice. Immediately I began investigating the quickest way to get a degree so I could throw up my shingle and get started. I needed to complete the BA first and then get into the two year Social Work program at McMaster while still working full time!

It was an exhilarating time. I remember walking on campus that first day in decades. I felt 19 in my head and I couldn't figure out why everyone was treating me as if I were 42! On my first trip to the library I just walked around with a dazed look in my eyes as I tried to absorb the volumes of information surrounding me. I was in awe of how much I did not know and at the same time, I was so anxious to learn!

Keep in mind that it had been 22 years since I had been in an academic environment. Sure I had taken the odd business course — but they had been nothing like this! I started coursework at McMaster University at the same time as Alexis was starting her first year at Western University. Between my job and the reading and essay writing my courses demanded, I basically worked all day and all night.

I would write the essays and then email them to Alexis so she could edit and proof read them. I got very good at writing and research so she thankfully didn't have to help her dear mother for too long!

The Social Work program I had entered was another ride into and through self-examination and discovery. Part of the coursework involved the dawning realization that most of the people who became helpers had been hurt repeatedly in their pasts.

There's a theory out there that suggests that knowing what it feels like to be at the rotten end of life is what makes for a good therapist. I think that might be true.

More importantly, I also believe that knowing what it feels like to be at the shiny end of life is a critically important characteristic of a great therapist. But I think what makes a therapist truly gifted is their ability to shine a light on the path that can take a person from rotten past to beautiful present, to be able to act as tour guide in the exploration of Life, and help people make the journey to their chosen destination with as much grace and ease as possible. That's the kind of therapist I would want for myself and that's the kind of therapist I long ago decided to be.

I never told myself that I couldn't go back to school because of my age. What a ridiculous excuse for not pursuing a dream! I knew what I wanted and I believed I could make it happen.

What I wasn't expecting was the ageism that was quite common in my university program. That surprised me, partly because I had really never thought anything of a person's age and certainly never attached judgment to their age. Unfortunately, that was not my experience in how others viewed and judged me. The irony didn't escape me either that we were in a social work program, supposedly focused on helping people, no matter who they were! If I heard the word 'oppression' once, I heard it a hundred times. It made me want to scream! That was the theme of social work a decade ago: the drive to relieve oppression.

Meanwhile, I was living it because of my age. At the beginning of the term, I was never asked to join a group. The Professor usually placed the 'stragglers' into groups. I remember being the fourth person in a group and the other three students talked amongst themselves and didn't even look at me. Even when we were on a break and just socializing, the younger students never approached me to chat.

The program involved a lot of group work and tons of writing so in a short time, the students around me learned that age had nothing to do with an A+ average. Aha!! Now everyone wanted me in their group! It brought me back to high school days when the popular kids got all the invitations.

At the end of the second year, everyone was required to do two three-month placements back-to-back which meant I would have no income for six months. So I planned and saved and decided to only have the essentials so I could be OK during that time.

The first placement was at Hickory House, which was a residential unit for young people with acquired brain injuries.

It was located at the psychiatric hospital on the mountain in Hamilton. It was the original hospital and it dated back to the days when we used to lock people up and throw away the key in many cases. Did you know that sometimes still happens today? The atmosphere was sterile, empty, and joyless. The first day there, I had to use the underground tunnel to walk from one section of the hospital to the entrance to the psych unit itself.

The tunnel smelled like anesthetic and it had tiny pink and green tiles on the walls — very shiny and sterile. I pushed the elevator button and waited. The door finally opened to reveal a food cart that no-one was pushing. Great! A bit spooked, I decided to use the stairs and found my way to Hickory House. I never used that tunnel again.

My three months at Hickory House were an amazing period of learning and expanding my awareness and skills. I speak often of some of the patients I worked with and what they taught me about life with a brain injury. More lessons! Does it ever end?

My second placement was in the Palliative Care program at St. Peter's hospital in Hamilton. It was my job to visit the patients daily and to visit with family members and help them move through the nightmare of red tape that accompanies the progression towards death. I learned there that you can ease into death or you can enter kicking and screaming but we all die.

Initially, it was difficult to understand how people could keep their sense of humour knowing they were dying soon. Then I realized that I was judging and stereotyping people based on their physical health.

When I started to see peoples' essences and who they were beyond the illness, it became easier and then, ultimately, I began to see it all as a gift. Some of the people I worked with were dying of brain cancer and either they didn't know who they were or they were living in some imaginary world. That was tough because their behaviour was usually out of control and marked by screaming, crying etc. But they were still human beings that responded to a soft voice, a gentle touch, or a few kind words.

There is great room in our world for compassion and the more tragedy I encountered in the lives of the people I met through my training, the less judgmental I found myself becoming. I finally graduated and started a consulting practice out of my home-based office. Today, 10 years later, I work out of an office in Burlington, Ontario, doing the counselling I love but also much more. I have expanded the services I provide to include meditation classes and workshops, and I host an internet radio program. I'm having fun! If someone had told me 15 years ago I would be doing this, I would have thought they were crazy. Lessons, more lessons!

Returning to school was an exciting adventure. I believed in the possibilities and had no doubts about what I was doing. I never met my mother-in-law but apparently one of her favourite sayings was "There is a `can' in `can't;' there is no 'will' in won't." I find with my clients that when they say 'I can't' it usually always means 'I won't'.

When I graduated, the school of Social Work said I could not open a private practice — it just wasn't done. I was shocked. The mainstream thought was that graduates would work for a government agency that addresses issues around poverty, oppression, and marginalization. Private practice was capitalism at its best! There was almost a shame attached to charging a fee for counselling services I clearly remember deciding to simply not tell people that I was opening a private practice — and although I thought the naysayers could be right, I decided that I would follow my dream anyway.

There was absolutely no way that I would be happy working in a government agency. It was my life; I was free to do with it whatever I wanted. And this was what I wanted. I think that's why I had no doubt.

Oh sure, I had *some* doubts about the number of clients I could see or how I would advertise, etc., because I lacked a business background. I had never been an entrepreneur and I really knew very little about being one. I had some business background from my management days in the pharmaceutical company but basically I learned everything from scratch.

Lesson # 3: Be Courageous

I could tell you that there were three major lessons I learned and yet I have difficulty with that. I believe that the lessons continue to unfold as we mature and see our lives and priorities unfolding around us. Awareness and insights grow with age. No matter what happens "to us" there is always a part of those experiences that are happening "for us," and they constitute the lessons we need to learn about ourselves.

Often we don't want to see or learn from the lesson because it's much easier to be a victim. Let me tell you a story. I was giving a talk to a group of people on bullying behaviour and respecting boundaries.

In the back of the room, there was a small group of people who were making comments that were a bit off-colour. I could hear them in the back but couldn't make out what they were saying. The woman sitting in front of them could hear them quite clearly and complained to upper management about their behaviour.

At first I laughed it off and thought she was exaggerating the events and then I realized this was an opportunity for me to learn and I looked for a lesson in the situation.

I had been working on speaking up, saying my truth with no apologies. I have long lived a life where speaking up was not encouraged. In fact, at times, it was downright dangerous. The lesson for me the day of my talk was that I needed to courageously speak up and have that loud little group show much more respect for the people around them and for me. Lesson learned—voilà done.

Another big "Aha!" moment was when I started to become aware of my positive and negative "triggers." Once I recognized a trigger, I drilled down to get to the underlying emotion or feeling and then further drilling led to the thought. Everything starts from a thought, even when you don't think there is one there. There is always a genesis. My genesis was "I am not good enough or worthy enough." I can't tell you how old that is but it goes way back into my history.

Here's the fascinating thing: this thought pattern was at the root of everything in my life. The kicker is that it was in disguise.

Like an invisible woman driving a bus — you're heading down the road but have no clue why you are making certain choices or why you are so damned angry all the time.

When you combine low self-worth with not speaking up, you get a pressure cooker of pent up anger and resentments; making decisions from this vantage point is never a good idea, sister. Here's the good news: you can stop it.

No one can provide you with self-worth or the feeling that you are more than good enough. In fact, you are spectacular! When we look to others to give us this, we are constantly disappointed and let down.

Marriages are often based on this. You might at first believe that he or she makes you feel so special and unique and loved but when your partner doesn't deliver, you fall into a really bad place.

What happens is that they now seem to be actually affirming that you are not worthy, and the cycle just keeps on going!

Be Courageous Reflections

Take some time right now and start writing without editing yourself. Allow your thoughts to flow freely as you think of these questions:

How aware are you of your judgments of others?

How has this stopped you from appreciating those people?

How do you judge yourself?

How do your self-judgments influence or dictate your actions?

Who do you judge the most?

Think of the most courageous moment in your life. How were you able to act courageously?

Chapter 4 — What Do You Want Me To Do, Yodel?

Everyone loves a love story and God knows, I am one of them. My sister told me that when I was little girl, I would wonder around the house planning my wedding, pretending it was about to happen, and dressing up as a bride.

As you may have gathered from my stories about ex-husbands my actual track record in the marriage department wasn't that hot.

Knowing what I know now, after being a therapist for 10 years, I can certainly explain why my marriages ended up in a heap. It's hard to be smart.

As I mentioned earlier, there was a time when I was going to university and still working a full time job.

Basically, all I did was work all the time. Despite that, I still liked to meet and be entertained by men so I joined the internet dating site Lavalife. It was great because I could screen the potential dates and cut down on a lot of potential time wasting moments.

My friends and family were all super cautious and everyone had heard TERRIBLE stories about women getting ripped off or worse, meeting an axe murderer! That was never my experience — the worst it got was death by boredom.

The company I was working for was planning a national sales meeting in London, England. Excited about the prospect of getting away from my life and enjoying a week in April in London, I logged on to Lavalife and typed in "Single men in London England" Up pops this man's picture and I immediately thought, "he looks so nice." So I sent him a message and immediately got an answer. I asked the safe question, "what's the weather like in jolly old" and he responded "Rain, rain, and more rain."

He then asked me my name and I responded "Heidi." He then wrote back "What do you want me to do, yodel?" To which I responded, "Noooo, that's my *name*." That nice looking man is now my husband.

Doug worked at a cable company just outside London and given the shifts and the time difference we spent three months talking to each other on a daily basis.

We talked about everything and laughed about more. My neighbour told me one night that it had been years since she heard laughter coming out of my house.

We made arrangements for Doug to fly over for a three-week vacation in Canada. I was so excited I couldn't sleep properly for days prior to his arrival.

I do like some flamboyance in my life so I decided to hire a stretch limo equipped with a fine bottle of Bordeaux. New dress, new shoes, perfect hair and nails.

I set off for the Toronto airport. Among the throngs of people waiting for passengers, I had sandwiched my way right up to the front of the railing and waited for what seemed to be forever. Finally, he walked through the doors with a smile so large, and a laugh so hearty I felt weightless.

My heart felt as if it were going to beat clear out of my chest. We ran around all the crowds and finally we met one another face to face. We kissed on the cheek and then walked as fast as we could, ducking and diving around the people to the limo. The car was parked in a special lot and I needed to call the driver to bring the car around. Fancy, right?

I was still so nervous that I couldn't remember how to work the cell phone so I gave it to Doug and asked him to call for the car. The limo pulled up and I looked at him and said, "Here's our car." Doug laughed and said "Sure it is," and I smiled and assured him that indeed it WAS our car! "Let's get in right now!"

We spent the next three weeks doing all the touristy stuff one does when you are only in a country for three weeks. But guess what? Doug never flew back to England. He arrived on August 12 and on August 22, we were married.

The Reverend who married us told us we needed to tell our story often because it is a good story with a happy ending. Reverend Tony is now deceased but I never forgot his advice.

On our wedding day, as part of the service, he gave us some more advice. He told me "Heidi, treat Doug as a King but not as a Queen, as a servant." "Doug, treat Heidi like a Queen, but not as a King, as a servant." We tried not to appear confused when we heard it and then we understood. When each partner comes from a place of equality and wants only what is best for the other partner, the results are magical.

As soon as the power shifts and one person is acting like royalty and looking down on the other, love and affection goes out the window. I remember those two pieces of advice from Rev. Tony and actually share them as many times as I can in the counselling process.

That part of the story is all about love and happy endings but there is also a dark part. In retrospect, I would have done things differently but, at the time I certainly felt I was justified in the decisions I made; however, those decisions caused a huge upheaval in my family.

Some relationships were completely severed and others severely disconnected. I have my own theories on why that happened but it doesn't matter now. What matters is that since then, the most important relationship has been healed.

In the meantime, I did choose the right partner for me and we continue to grow and learn about each other every day.

Lesson # 4 — Believe it-Feel it-Create It-Live it

The story you just read is missing the most important piece. How possible is it to create a situation just by envisioning it and feeling it? In other words, attracting into your life all that you want and wish to experience?

I say, it is completely possible — and here is why:

I don't believe in coincidences, instead I believe that everything happens in divine order and timing. I started to investigate the Law of Attraction about 11 years ago. It is a universal law just like the Law of Gravity— and we women know a thing or two about that law! The Law of Attraction, in its simplest form, states that we will get results wherever we direct our energy, attention, and focus.

The concept that we create our reality may be difficult for you to wrap your head around, but for the most part, where attention goes, energy flows and when our attention is focused on our desires, we manifest our desires.

Having said that, bad things happen and there are certain things that can only be controlled by God and understood as God's wishes. Even that concept for many is a difficult one and not one that I am going to talk about in this book!

What I would like to tell you about is what happened New Years Eve, 11 years ago:

My close friend Helena had lived through almost all of the same rocky dating relationships that I had experienced and we were both really tired of the emotional carnage. I was curious to put this Law of Attraction to the test, so Helena and I sat in the family room and we came up with a list of qualities that I wanted in my ideal partner.

We used our imaginations and the list was long. We included good conversationalist, dancer, reader, sense of humour and so on.

I would read this list every day and imagine and visualize what this man would look like.

I would also feel (and that's the key to the Law) how wonderful it would feel to be loved because I was in this universe — not because I was smart, successful, charming you name it — but just because of who I AM.

I removed all doubt and believed that at the right time and in divine order, the universe would deliver this match. This match is now my husband Doug. Less than 6 months after I created the list, we met online, 3,000 miles apart.

This is also part of the Law of Attraction that I find brilliant. If someone had told me that I would meet a man online, from another country, and get married I likely would have thought it unbelievable and not very likely!

What the Law teaches is that we take the 'how' and the 'when' out of our desires and open ourselves to the enormous possibilities of 'perhaps'. That is where the magic happens.

Although I first started reading about the Law 11 years ago, now I am living it. I am a full time student with a Law of Attraction Professor and I am learning to live my life in belief.

I am wildly open to living a life open to receiving, to allowing, knowing that we are limitless, and being in joy.

Believe it — Feel it — Create it — Live it Reflections

Take some time right now and start writing without editing yourself. Allow your thoughts to flow freely as you think of these questions:

What would your life look like if you believed anything was possible?

When we are kids, daydreams are our life and adults drill that out of us. What would it be like if you started to daydream again?

Chapter 5 — Mast under Rocks

The boat's name was Gamin. She was a dream come true for my husband as he had assumed possession of the 15-foot keeled dinghy for free and he couldn't believe his luck. This keel business was apparently quite important and impressive. The free business struck me as something akin to being given a basket of kittens. Free indeed.

My husband was originally from England, a place where only the very well-heeled could afford to sail. When he moved to Ontario, his longing for a sailboat lurched from "impossible" to "maybe someday" and he insisted on dragging me along for the ride.

Doug wanted his own boat. In our early days together, we would hold hands and stand beside each other down by Lake Ontario and envision our own sailboat. We could see her in our minds' eyes, a gorgeous boat with white billowy sails. I was a pretty part of the picture too, with a snazzy white cable knit sweater and rolled up blue jeans.

I would hand the Skipper a glass of wine as we merrily sailed around the lake — heck maybe around an ocean? (Why contain imagination? It was, after all, just a dream at that point!)

You get what you focus on and sure enough, a call came in one day from a gentleman who had heard of my husband's dream. The man was moving to Asia and he wanted someone to haul the boat, trailer, new sails and accessories out of his garage and taken away. It was a freebie.

Doug's dream had come true in spades! I, on the other hand, was not quite as excited. As some of my acquaintances well know, I have an acute fear of drowning and I am therefore wary of boats. Even when I had my kayak, I was a fair weather paddler. If the wind was too strong I stayed on land.

My fear hadn't held me back, however; I had, in fact, been sailing with my husband before, although always in the company of sailors with more experience than either one of us. I had always wondered why Doug moved so quickly in a boat. Most of the sailors I had been out with moved deliberately but moderately. There was a peaceful rhythm to their movements that Doug simply did not share. He would rush and race to do everything at once, his excitement getting the better of him at every turn. This made me nervous but I was willing to be part of the adventure. I am an adventurous gal.

So after the new boat had been delivered, Doug spruced his new darling up (the boat, not me) and we decided to take her out for a spin. It was a delightful day.

The wind was gentle, the sun was shining and it wasn't long before I could see myself in that white cable knit sweater again. When we got back home I would have to find out where to purchase one. Life was *that* good! Sitting calmly like a lady of leisure should, I looked up into the sky and sighed peacefully before noticing that there was a metal line flapping happily out behind the boat in the gentle summer breeze.

"What is that flapping Doug?" I asked. The look on his face said it all. I instantly began imagining me and my white sweater bobbing aimlessly but upright in Hamilton Bay. Dead, of course, either through boating mishap or the toxic quality of the water in that area. Hamilton is home to many steel mills and the water proves it.

Doug swung into excited action. He shouted "It's the halyard that's come loose – grab it!"

"Well," I thought, "that's not so bad." It was an illusion I was able to maintain until I looked up and noticed that the mast had begun to bend. The longer it took me to grab the halyard the more the mast was bending. Now I pictured myself face up with white cable knit sweater in stinky polluted water with a mast through my chest.

But it was no time for fear. I leaned over the side of the boat and somehow managed to keep steady enough to grab the errant metal line and start screwing it back into its place. I did it! The danger was over and I sat down, prepared to refocus on enjoying the tranquility you always see in sailing ads. That was not to be the case because the halyard came untied again!

"Once more onto the breech, woman," I thought valiantly. I grabbed that sucker and tightened it as hard as I could.

At that point we decided to head for safe harbour. That experience was enough for me to realize that the boat obviously hated me. It was clearly telling me I had no business pretending to be comfortable — sweater or no.

A few weeks passed and I decided that maybe I had been too hasty. How can a boat hate someone anyway? Wasn't I bigger than that? So off we went for another adventure. It was a windier day than it had been the last time we had ventured out with Gamin, and Doug had a huge problem getting the sail up the mast. It was as if the boat were saying, "Oh no you don't!" and we were saying "Oh yes we do!"

Doug kept heaving and jerking and finally the sail made it to the top of the mast. Married Couple One, Boat Zero. Now keep in mind that the wind was blowing in from the North East and I knew from my kayaking days that easterly winds are unnatural. In fact, I never took my kayak out in an east wind — way too risky! Standing on the dock, my intuition began screaming at me. (Note to self: always trust your gut!)

"DO NOT GET ON THAT BOAT!!!!!!" it hollered. But when I looked at Doug's face and saw how excited he was, how eager to live out the dream of sailing his own vessel, I softened. We all need dreams.

So, against my highly evolved and intelligent inner mind, I decided to give it a whirl. We cast off. Stealing wickedly through the marina like a thief on a tight schedule, the wind grabbed the sail, taking us both by surprise. Doug had to tack fast — and as I mentioned he was usually pretty quick on the uptake — but unfortunately, he lost control of the boat and we capsized. I was now living my worst nightmare. Gone were the visions of peace, sunsets, wine, and white cable knit sweaters and here instead was the reality of my body floating in the Bay with a useless boat for company. Doug and I were both shocked and treading water like mad.

Doug knew he had to right the boat by getting up on the keel that was now lurching above his head at a right angle to the water. This boat was big but after much manly effort he clambered onto the keel, confident that his weight would re-balance the boat back to its natural upright stance. It didn't work. There was absolutely no way he could right the boat. I don't want to make this all sound so easy. At the time, we were flailing around in the water like chickens at a stir-fry.

Doug was shouting instructions and I couldn't think straight. Slowly (probably much faster than I thought) people started to come down to the waterfront and they rallied around us helpfully. Someone eventually realized that the mast was caught under some of the rocks that peppered the shoreline of the marina area and that there was no way we could have righted the boat using the traditional "stand on the keel" method.

Slowly, helpful people pitched in and started to take bits of the lines and unravel them from the mast so it could be freed from the rocks.

I was getting tired of treading water and just wanted to get out onto dry land. It took me quite a while to realize there was an easy way to do that: just stand up. That's right folks, we were still in the marina and neither Doug nor I realized that all we had to do was stand up and walk to shore. It was quite embarrassing.

Once the mast situation was sorted out, we walked to the dock. The helpful folks on dry land asked us politely if we were OK but didn't get into too much of a flap over our misadventure. They considered the experience to be simply part of acquiring sailing knowledge and experience. At the time I figured my life would probably be complete if I never stepped foot in that wicked boat again. And I never did. Was there a lesson in all that?

Yes! Go to school! Yup It wasn't enough that I could never get the black marks out of my drenched T-shirt again but then Doug convinced me that all we needed was a "proper" sailing course from the Canadian Yachting Association. Wonderful. The course unrolled over three full weekends of classroom and on-water instruction. It would definitely improve our sailing skills but I wasn't confident it would improve my trust in sailing.

The first two weekends went great. We learned a lot about what everything was called on the boat— although now, strangely, I only remember the word "halyard." We learned how to tie knots, start the motor and deal with a man overboard (God help us).

We weren't in trouble until the last weekend As soon as we stepped outside the front doors of our condo I noticed whitecaps on the lake — usually a sign that the wind is strong. Remember — I am the person who wouldn't go out in her kayak if the leaves on the trees were rustling even slightly. By the time we got to the marina I was certain the instructor would call the whole thing off. Oh, no, not a chance. Instead the whole class piled into the boat the instructor had selected for us.

We all felt nervous since the only people with any experience were my husband (a.k.a Mr. Dump-Us-In-the-Marina) and the instructor, who by this time was standing comfortably below us in the galley, shouting instructions at us above the roar of the wind.

You can guess what happened. We all froze. Except for Doug, and that's only because the instructor yelled at him most of all since he was the only student with sailing experience. He did it all on his own with the shouted instructions from the teacher. At that point, Doug became my hero and I forgave him for all the previous mishaps. None of that mattered now.

We clung close to shore hoping we would escape the wind. NOT A CHANCE! It was bedlam. Finally, the instructor ordered the storm jib up and we managed to get back to safe harbour. I was bedraggled and exhausted and quite certain I did not enjoy sailing very much.

No one can say I didn't give it my best shot, though! Voilà done! I knew I would never be in a sailboat again and good luck to all the sailors out there. I did actually graduate from that sailing class — as a mate, though, not as a skipper. Whew! Another one under the belt!

The story doesn't quite end there, however, much as it probably should. I've never been one to keep a good yarn under my hat and when my daughter Alexis got hold of the news of our misadventure, she just couldn't leave it alone. I guess the apple doesn't fall far from the tree. At the time, Alexis was busy having adventures of her own and she seized upon the thread of my sailing catastrophe and wove it into a tapestry all of her own making. She generously allowed me to include her account of the place my sailing career had in her life in this book , and I've reprinted it below. Of course I find her twist on my "Tragedy" much funnier now than I did at the time. Time heals all wounds, I guess, even the ones that hurt our pride.

And now, a story from my daughter...

My Classy Mother

By Alexis Bergamo:

I struggle to find a starting point for this story and of course there is so much to tell: I had been married, my heart had been ripped out of my chest (not literally of course, but don't tell my 26-year old self that), I had been divorced, and of course I had fallen back in love again. Oddly, this all has something to do with my mother (what doesn't?).

When the New Man said he wanted to travel, to see the world, to get out of this god-forsaken town, I was completely on board. After all, running away from the life I used to lead sounded like a holiday I'd like to live for awhile instead of visiting and inevitably having to relinquish it all. As it turned out, my plans for a one-year stint in Europe with the New Man turned into a nearly-four-year adventure all over the other side of the world. What a journey it's been!

The original plan was that Craig and I would travel to Italy and find work there as teachers. Unfortunately, employment was hard to come by for those without a coveted EU passport, but the search became easier the further east one was willing to look.

In January, Craig announced he had settled on Korea and he urged me to pack my bags and join him. I made the decision in mid-February while on an impromptu road trip through Texas, of all places. Giant billboards encouraging me to "Go there, Lex" kept appearing at the side of the road. I was sure that this was a sign, not for a war memorial at Lexington, but for me to leave this place (North America) and venture out to the Great East. I announced to my family that I would be going with Craig to Korea. My father's response was priceless. "Asia? **You can't go to Asia**!" he exclaimed.

That settled it: I was going.

I wonder sometimes if I was truly just running from the past or if I was simply trying to prove something to myself and to my people. "My people" included family and friends at that point, although the term would come to mean something completely different one year later. Perhaps I wanted to show that I could do something amazingly risky; something way outside of the Hamilton, Ontario, life that I had signed up for when I had said, "I do." Either way, I was determined that this would be a risk worth taking. I thoroughly researched the school systems and the culture and I packed my two enormous suitcases with every single prized possession I owned. I was ready to join Craig, who had left four months earlier, and eager to start our awesome year of Korean living.

Before I get to the hilarity of the airport, let me first say that Craig and I had only talked once — via Skype — the whole time he had been off in Korea.

Once.

I knew it was over and I knew the dream of "happily ever after" was never going to happen for us. But I went anyway. I thought that once I was there, he would remember "the magic" and we'd start the romantic montage I'd been daydreaming about for four months. Somewhere deep down though, I knew it wouldn't work out. Upon careful reflection, I realized that was probably why I went: I needed to get away from the people who loved me so that I could grieve on my own the knowledge that there wasn't a man waiting for me.

I had to independently prepare to withstand yet another paralyzing blow to my ego, my heart, my life. It was time for some autonomy and time to feel this debilitating pain, again.

The journey to Korea was not routine, but who would have thought it would have been? My luggage was overweight and I was completely broke, so my father had to bail me out. I was so embarrassed. Then, because I was stopping over in Chicago before continuing on to Seoul, I had to go through US Customs in the Toronto airport.

My parents had no idea the mayhem that was about to unfold as they waved goodbye to their only offspring. When asked on the customs form if I was bringing in any weapons, fruits, seeds, meat, animal products, weapons of mass destruction, terrorists, or live Ethiopian babies, I replied frankly, "No." The muffins my mother had made for the trip were in plain sight. And so were the cherries she'd lovingly washed and wrapped.

Again I was prodded, "Are you sure you don't have any of these products?"

"Nope," said rather glibly.

"No seeds or fruit?"

A strange look upon my face followed by a slow and steady, "Noooo?"

I was asked to step into The Room on the Left. Do whatever you can to avoid The Room on the Left. It's where baby-kidnappers and machine-gun builders go when customs officers are sure they're the Bad Guys.

And now, I was one of them. I didn't understand the gravity of my situation until forty minutes after arriving, some forty-five minutes after seeing my parents for the last time for twelve months; I was called to the booth to "explain myself." I still thought this was a big misunderstanding and, in fact, I had eaten most of my flax seed-riddled muffins and was about to dive into the cherries...oh god. There are pits in the cherries. And seeds in the muffins. Seeds. In. the. Muffins. Clearly visible from the outside of their cellophane wrapper. What an idiot.

"I'm terribly sorry, Sir," I choked out. "I didn't even realize I had these. My mom made them for my trip over to Korea and when the man asked if I had any seeds, I naturally said no because I don't have any seeds and then I realized that I had a lot of seeds...there are seeds all over the place in my hands right now and I completely realize now what I've done wrong and..."

The customs officer cut me off.

"Young lady, you lied to a United States Customs Officer. Do you know what the fine is for such an offence?"

Offence? Come on. I just forgot about some damn seeds! Cherries! Since when are cherries a crime?!

"No, Sir."

"$200 to start with, but we can certainly detain you for an appropriate period of time."

Well now I was sweating. My mouth was dry. I was on the brink of tears when I simply blurted out, "I'm moving to Korea to be with a guy who probably doesn't even want to be with me anymore. I'm completely out of money so much so that my father just had to pay the Korean Air lady so that I could take all my precious belongings with me to a foreign country. I have nothing and I can't give you anything. I have nothing left." I was drained. I was tired. I was dejected. And the journey had only just begun.

He gave me a stern warning and let me go. I walked so briskly away from the kidnappers and bomb-assemblers, it was a miracle I didn't trip. If this was any indication of how the next 365 days were going to play out, I was certainly in for a wild (read: awful) ride. Lessons learned: Read Carefully and Don't be afraid to admit defeat. In hindsight, though I had "nothing," I still had an enormous amount of gumption. And that's really something.

Korea certainly wasn't easy for me. The first week was lonely and fully challenging at every step. Craig and I confirmed the fact that we would share no future together and I faced the prospect of making a life for myself with dismal determination. One of my work colleagues was assigned to the task of taking me under his wing both at school and with regards to my apartment, and because he was a decent, loving man, the effort of making that teeny tiny place my own was far easier. He became known as My Man very soon thereafter and I am to this day eternally grateful for the time and energy he invested in my ignorant, intolerant self.

There was one other person who made a big impact on my life in Korea, someone who showed me the intricacies of traditional Korean life, and taught me that being gentle and open allows for empathy and acceptance. Mrs. Lim (pronounced, "Yim"), became known as my Korean Mother and she was instrumental in my transition from narrow-minded, belligerent foreigner, to the woman who would grow to call Asians, "My People." With grace and pride, she brought me into her culture and begged to know more, more, ever more about mine. She tended to me when I was sick; she brought me to the swine flu clinic and held my disease-riddled hand while a nurse stuck a probe so high up my nose I could swear it touched my brain; she cooked **piles** of food early in the morning, boxed it, and then carted it all with her on the hour-long bus ride right to my house; she picked up my favourite pumpkin soup with black beans when I called in sick for the umpteenth time in a month; and she introduced me to my first Asian acupuncturist. I trusted her implicitly and I was eager to help her in any way I could.

Many of our conversations about North American culture centred on food, and at one point I told Mrs. Lim about my mother's disdain for the expression, "I'm full." Finding this quite odd, Mrs. Lim needed to know more.

I started the story: "When I was twelve, my mother planned a very ornate, beautiful trip across the Rockies from Banff to Victoria, British Columbia. It was a breathtaking adventure that changed my Mom at every twist and turn of the road. I was completely oblivious to the beauty, however, or so my mother thought, because I was twelve and vile and wanted to be at home with my best friend, talking about boys and hair styles."

This she could not believe: how could anyone not want to experience the splendour of the Rockies? This woman had two very normal children who, I'm sure, would have felt exactly the same way, but Korean culture necessitated that they never speak or act disrespectfully to their elders, rendering poor Mrs. Lim completely oblivious to the fact that **her** twelve-year-old kids were just like twelve-year-old **me**: awful.

I continued. "One night, we ate a poignantly delicious meal at a fondue restaurant of sorts. I was a young, growing girl and I ate all the meat I could possibly manage, with the result that I was on cloud nine for the first time since the start of the trip, I leaned back, put my hands on my engorged belly and replied, 'I'm FULL!' Well, my mother was having **no** part in that. She adamantly stuck up her index finger, waved it defiantly in my face, and said, "You do NOT say, 'I'm full', young lady, you say, 'I'm SATISFIED', all the while shaking her head disapprovingly."

Well that hit Mrs. Lim in all the right places. She was beaming: my mother was just like her! "Your mother is so classy!" she said.

And so it began: my mother was classy because she got rid of two coffee mugs after getting new ones as gifts instead of letting the extra clutter her cupboards; she was classy because she planned dinner menus by cutting out recipes and table setting options from magazines; she was classy because she "had her colours done," a service I don't even think Mrs. Lim fully understood. It's not that I don't agree with Mrs. Lim: my mother **is** classy. It's just that My Korean Mother had a bit of a lady crush on my actual mother and it was pretty hilarious. Everything my mother did was classy in some way, shape, or form. Until one day...

As I'm sure you've read in this book, my mother had a (ahem) "near death experience" involving The Boat in the Burlington Bay while I was in Korea. Because I knew she had had an **actual** near-death experience involving water, I was all-ears to hear the telling of this harrowing tale after it first occurred.

Fresh were her wounds as she regaled me with a real-time account of how she – **my one and only Mother!** — nearly died! I listened intently, sure that she must have been calling me from the hospital, and I was poised to come home on the next Korean Air flight out of Seoul. And then my mother delivered the punch line: the water in the marina was actually only four feet deep and she was easily able to stop treading water while fearing for her life and simply stand up. All was just fine in the land of skippers and captains. Oh, we did have a laugh about that one. And I, in true I-do-love-telling-a-great-story fashion, immediately told my expat friends in Korea. Pealing with laughter, I knew I had a keeper.

The following day, I told Mrs. Lim that I had a vexing tale about My Classy Mother to tell her from that weekend.

"It is a doozy," I said.

"Doozy? What doozy?"

"Never mind. There's no time to explain. Prepare yourself."

I launched in, careful to ensure that my facial expressions completely and utterly surpassed all levels of fright from the original tale. Emotions mounted to horror status as Mrs. Lim inched further and further toward the edge of her chair, now fully in the know about Mom's childhood water scare. She was on her feet when I told her about the sailboat ("See? Your mother is **so** classy!") and the adventures of getting certified to sail it.

"And brave, too! She so brave!" Oh brother. Was there no end to her devotion?

At long last, the moment of truth was upon us: the finale. Of course the best part for Mrs. Lim was not the end of a joke, but rather the climax, the pinnacle, the reason for her current standing and punching [punching!] stance. Her eyebrows were raised high, and her tiny Asian body tensed in a wide-legged, fight-or-flight position, her fists were clenched and her jaw was tight, when I told her:

"And then the man on the shore yelled, 'Why don't you just stand up?' and she **did**! She was in *four feet of water*! Bwhahahahaahaha." My enjoyment was immense.

But Mrs. Lim, oh Mrs. Lim was another story. She literally collapsed. Well, she didn't actually **fall**, but her whole demeanour plunged: her eyebrows remained raised, poised to accept that this could not possibly be the end. Her dreams, her classy lady crush...this couldn't be happening. She straightened, brushed off her trousers, and relaxed the tension in her face at long last. She was frazzled, I could tell. Perhaps telling a joke about my mother wasn't the thing to do. Did she find me insulting? What did I want her to say? "Ohhh...not so classy anymore!?" Was I just awfully cruel about my own Mother? Oh dear. I'd made a crucial error.

And then the corners of her mouth curled up slowly, creeping dangerously toward what could only be described as a grin-grimace hybrid. She pointed at me and said in a clear mysterious voice,

"Your mother is **still VERY** classy."

Lesson # 5 — Hope through Fear

The power of intention and the results we get when we harness our energies with others to focus on a desire, turns that desire into reality.

Thought takes form on some level and the power of visualization, combined with focus, and declaring our intentions to God and the Universe, creates our reality.

We attracted Gamin into our lives — as Alexis had attracted Korea — and sure, it wasn't the exact situation any of us had visualized but it was a match to our intentions, focus, and energy.

Intuition. The inner mind is innately more clever and powerful than the outer mind (also known as our ego) yet we choose to deny our intuition and rationalize.

Think of that word "rationalize" — notice how it transforms awfully easily into the words "ration-lies." Does that support us in our daily lives? No!

And think about this: we never ask our heart to beat, our blood to pump or our lungs to breathe. That all happens continuously without any input from our rational, conscious mind.

The Universe has everything worked out to perfect order and the more we pay attention to that little voice that might be saying a version of "Don't get on that boat!" the richer our lives will become.

Passion. The sail boat became a symbol of many things. The mast holds up the main sail, which is the engine of the boat. It determines the shape of the sail, how fast we move and in what direction we travel.

The mast is like our life's purpose and all of our passion. It's the strength that holds all of our actions together to produce an outcome.

I witnessed Doug's passion for sailing and could identify with it when I compared it to my passion for kayaking. His whole demeanour, outlook, and perspective were so positive and healthy when he was able to sail – when he was able to live his passion. When we lose sight of our purpose and passion we stop moving and we are trapped under the rocks of despair.

Sometimes we need people in our lives to unravel the ropes of despair and confusion that we wrap ourselves in. They inspire us to move into a state of freedom where it is safe to explore and stand upright and re-focus ourselves with passion and purpose.

Kindness. I witnessed the kindness and gentleness of people around me when I needed help the most and realized that their acts of giving were done with nothing expected in return.

Their purpose was to help fellow sailors. That might be because they have been there themselves, or could be one day. But there was no judgment – just pure gentle spirit and understanding.

*"**The secret of life is to fall seven times and get up eight**" — **Paulo Coelho***

One tour of duty in the bay and the marina was enough for me. I will leave the sailing to those who truly love the feeling of the wind and the chic of those white cable knit sweaters.

I will take a hike in the park!

Hope Through Fear Reflections

Take some time right now and start writing without editing yourself. Allow your thoughts to flow freely as you think of these questions:

What stops you from trusting your intuition?

What stops you from living your purpose and passion?

How aware are you of your purpose and passion?

What in your life creates doubt?

What old messages are you still carrying around?

What self-limiting beliefs are holding you back?

Chapter 6: Get Off the Train, Get on the Right Track

Some of the best lessons in my life came in the wake of a two-week vacation my husband and I enjoyed in Italy one year.

Both of us had travelled extensively throughout Europe before and we agreed that Italy was a dream destination. Everything there was perfect. Except for the train system. After the flight to Milano we had to take a cab to the train station and then take the train to Genoa, with a transfer to Cinque Terra.

We were sitting on the benches at the Milan train station, jet lagged and dog tired, of course, and this train pulls up beside us. All announcements were in Italian, which was a bit of a hindrance since we didn't speak the language. We sat calmly together on our bench and I looked at hubby with drowsy eyes and said,

"Do you think that is our train?"

"I dunno," he answered, "Do you think it's our train?"

"Hmmm...maybe. I will ask that kid hanging out the window." So I did, and as the train slowly started to move, the kid yelled out "Yes, and this is the last train to Cinque Terra." Now I am running (picture Charlie's Angels style) and banging on the side of the train in the vain hope that it would stop. The train left.

Plan B was now in effect. We learned that another train was due to leave in an hour so we waited and soon enough, the train pulled into the station – early. "Aha!" we thought, ``this is our train finally, and it's on time—bonus! We raced on board and settled our belongings. I looked around at the people on the train and had a funny feeling this was not the right train. So I asked and intuition was right! Off we jumped.

Finally the right train pulled in and we dozed comfortably off and on during the three-hour journey to our destination, Riomaggiore, **in** Cinque Terra. Riomaggiore is the most southern town in the chain that compiles Cinque Terra. We rented an adorable 2 bedroom apartment and it became our base camp. Every day we would venture off to a new location.

Cinque Terra is a UNESCO Heritage Site and consists of 5 villages scattered between the sea coastline and the mountains. The main tourist attraction is the hiking path that connects all villages. Unfortunately, the path had been washed out by the winter avalanche and in true Italian style, no one knew or cared when it would be repaired. The only other way to see the towns was by boat and train and we opted for both experiences.

Once we got over the jet lag, my husband and I dedicated ourselves to figuring out how the train system worked and after some intense research we realized that they were usually late or on strike. We never bothered to buy tickets as a result, because on the "Regionale" you could purchase them on board.

What made our trip especially exciting was that my daughter, Alexis, was joining us in Riomaggiore for three days. She was teaching in London, England, and passing through for a two-week vacation in Spain. It was magical! We had all headed off for a lovely day trip in Santa Margarita. Santa Margarita is a coastal town on the Golfo dei Poeti – Poet's Gulf aptly named for the history of English poets and writers that made Santa Margarita their home.

I understood why they found inspiration in this delightful town. The streets were lined with giant palm trees. Lemons on the lemon trees were a vivid yellow colour and bursting with aroma. Bougainvillea plants were popping with fuchsia pink blossoms.

Families strolled along the sea wall and children played in the piazza. The three of us wandered around town and walked into the next town using the back roads to get a real feel for the Italian lifestyle. The houses were mostly white stucco with window boxes spilling out red and pink geraniums. The houses were carved into the mountainsides and terraced gardens embellished the scene. Any flat piece of land held a garden or a vineyard. Lemon trees just seemed to grow out of the side of the mountains and there were bushes of rosemary everywhere. Feeling very deserving after a long hike one day, we sat down to a delicious meal of scallops — just caught — pasta, red wine and bread.

As we arrived back at the station we realized that — voilà! — the train was already there waiting for us.

What a perfect day! We ran like crazy to catch it, knowing we could buy the tickets on board.

As we settled into our places, I noticed how different this train was from the other regional trains we'd been on. There were tables, soft seats, internet connections. Something was not right. As I was trying to put the pieces together, Alexis struck up a conversation with a sweet couple sitting opposite us. They were busy with their laptops and they told Alexis that they were Masters students living in Florence. My 29 year old daughter was a bit intimidated since living in Florence sounded much more worldly than visiting for three days. With your parents.

As the conversation continued, I could see the conductor walking down the aisle. She had a cap on her head. It was very snappy looking but this, too, seemed very unusual. The conductor stopped at our seats and asked for our tickets. We explained, poorly, that we thought we could buy them on the train. She looked at us as if we were THE stupidest people God ever created but she had a heart. She explained, badly, that we would have to pay 140 Euros to take the 20 minute trip to our destination. We were on the Eurostar, after all! Case solved. We were on the most expensive train in Italy. Heck, this was probably the most expensive train in all of Europe!

She then shouted "Get off now!" We felt a bit puzzled.

"Now?" we asked.

"Yes, right now — get off right now!"

We quickly gathered our belongings, ran to the door and got off the train. My daughter was mortified since the whole time the students from Florence had been looking on as if we were indeed THE stupidest people on the planet. Let's face it, at 29 years of age it matters what people think of us. As soon as we started to walk clear of the train, Alexis began asking me, repeatedly, how I could not be embarrassed!

Really I thought the whole thing was funny. It was never our intention to get away without paying so as long as our intentions are right and pure then there was nothing to be embarrassed about.

Lesson #6: —Get on the Right Track

I often use different aspects of my train story as an analogy to illustrate different lessons. Sharing my own experiences as a teaching tool shows others where I once was vis-à-vis where I am today in my approach to life. I believe it makes me more real and less of an 'expert.' (Experts can get tedious, can't they?)

Years ago, I realized that one huge fear kept me chained to myself: the fear of scarcity and lack. No matter how well I did at something or how lovely a person was towards me, my inner voice would insist that it would never last, that I wasn't good enough, smart enough, rich enough, or just "enough," period. I was always getting in my own way! So I went to see my psychic and spiritually intuitive friend (who also knows how to bust my chops), and, with a hand on my forehead Scarlett O'Hara-style I asked (with a Southern drawl)

"When will this all stop?"

Priya then said, as sweetly as possible "When you stop it." Aha! Don't you just love those moments of complete clarity and vision? Especially when they're delivered along with a good dose of humour!

Because my default position has always tended to be one of lack, fear, and scarcity, I now visualize a train going forward on a track with two canyons on either side of me. One canyon is the "fear canyon" and the other is the "lack," or "scarcity canyon."

I just don't allow myself to veer off into either canyon and it can take a lot of corrections to keep me going straight ahead. Less now that I am used to the process, but when I started, I was constantly correcting. As soon as I felt the train wobble to one side, I would correct.

I know, you are thinking, "That's easier said than done!"

I would agree — it is not easy to think something new and different when every cell in your body wants to go back to default. Back to what you believe to be true.

I think that what stops many of us from moving from here to there —is the belief that "this is so hard!" As long as we continue to believe something is hard, it will feel impossible. If you believe it will be possible, then you open the doors to all possibilities.

Once we believe in the possibilities we then need to open ourselves to receiving. Receiving can show up in all sorts of different ways: compliments, generous gestures or words, help, support, understanding and compassion.

Some people have difficulty opening themselves to receiving because there is an underlying feeling of lack of self-worth. If we feel undeserving, then opening to receiving is uncomfortable. What people frequently tell me — from their heads — is, "of course I am deserving," because they *think* they are; but they do not *feel* they are worthy.

If you are wondering how you truly feel, look around at your world and see how your life is a reflection of your self-worth. Are you surrounded by pretty things? Is there money in your bank account? How fulfilling are your relationships? How lovingly does your partner treat you? How enriching are your friendships?

What you are physically experiencing in your life is a reflection of how you *feel* about yourself. Every feeling produces a vibration and we can only have one vibration at a time. Emotions are energy in motion so when we feel sad we are vibrating at a low energy frequency. Conversely, when we are feeling joyful we are vibrating at a high frequency. You will attract more of what you are vibrating!

Get On the Right Track Reflections:

Take some time right now and start writing without editing yourself. Allow your thoughts to flow freely as you think of these questions:

Where is your train headed?

How deserving do you truly feel?

Look at your life and write down the evidence of your self-worth

How are you experiencing lack?

How are you experiencing abundance?

What or whom is stopping you from getting on the right track?

What or whom do you need to release?

Chapter 7 — The Wheels on the Bus

To celebrate my husband's 55th birthday we took a cruise that brought us to the Mayan Rivera, Grand Cayman, and Belize. Part of the draw for me was the chance to see the Mayan ruins of Caracol in Belize, so we booked it as one of our on-shore trips. Belize is recognized as the centre of the ancient Maya world. Here, in the "central lowlands" of western Belize and in the Guatemalan area of Petén, the ancient Maya flourished during the Classic Period from 300 to 900 AD. Archaeologists now estimate that 2,000,000 Mayans once lived in what is now Belize.

Humbling history aside, we were about to stumble into an adventure.

When it came time for our excursion, my husband and I boarded the tour bus and waited some time before the last two passengers finally made it on board. Keep in mind that it was 9:00 AM and the last fellow to lurch into our merry company of tourists was drunk and also carrying one more beer for the road. Maybe more than one more. He was a likeable drunk, funny and entertaining. For most of the trip, he sat in the back, giggling with his girlfriend.

The drive took us through streets and neighbourhoods that were surprisingly poor and remote.

Touch the Whale

Previously, when I had thought of Belize, I had conjured up the type of image I'd seen in travel folders and on web sites. None of that presented itself on this trip! Despite the lackluster scenery, it was still pleasant to be on vacation and experiencing new surroundings with no stress. Well, it was pleasant and stress-free until the bus broke down.

By this time, it was about 85 degrees and we were told we needed to wait for another bus. It wasn't that the engine had conked out — it was just that the air conditioning had given up the ghost.

The driver gave us a choice: we could complete the trip with the windows open or wait for another bus to pick us up. Unanimously, we all opted for option B and we settled down to wait for another bus.

We must have been quite a sight, waiting there at the side of the road. Buses do not come quickly in Belize. There wasn't much to look at: a couple of pastures with weary looking horses, goats, and cows. Cats and dogs that wandered by as if to say "Are you guys crazy?" The only person who was somewhat prepared for all eventualities was Mr. Boozy, who just kept drinking beer. This seemed like a sensible thing to do on a hot day in the Caribbean! At long last, the rescue bus appeared and we piled on to a delightfully cold bus for the rest of the journey.

When we arrived at our destination there was a bloom of sacredness surrounding the ruins. It was clear that the tourist guides were proud of this site and they made it equally clear to us visitors that we needed to stay on the designated pathways. No garbage of any kind was to be left behind. (I'm not too sure where Mr. Boozy's empty beer cans went...)

There was a certain irony in all this since a rock band had recently received approval to perform their concert on the grounds of the ruins. I guess no-one was afraid the sound would disturb the peace at all. Hmmm.

It was delightful to wander through the grounds and to get a feel of the energy of the land and of the people. Eventually we made our way to the temple we had come to see. We knew that from the top we would have an amazing view of the surrounding jungle countryside.

There were staircases on each side of the temple and since they were the originals, they were tiny, steep and seemingly endless. My husband and I stepped carefully one after another and finally made it to the top for the glorious view. The rest of the tour group joined us, except for one man who was having a hard time making his way up the narrow incline. Yup. Mr. Boozy — who was still boozy at this point. We all stood at the top of the temple, almost holding our breath and hoping this guy would make it all the way without falling.

Remarkably, he made it. He smiled widely at everyone and then walked calmly over to the edge without trepidation or fear. My husband then asked him what he thought of the view. Mr. Boozy stretched his arms straight out beside him and in a booming voice cried "OUTSTANDING!"

We all laughed but he captured what we were all thinking: it was outstanding! I always feel so blessed and yet at the same time overwhelmed when I am in the midst of pure beauty and spirit. There is something very humbling about standing on ground that has survived way longer than I ever will or, for that matter, ground that will outlast any human. It's astounding how we ascribe so much importance and self-importance to the daily strivings of our life. In comparison to the magnificence around me in the Mayan ruins, it all seemed very small – significant yet small.

We all managed to get back down the stairs to the ground and by that time, it was time to return to the tour bus and back to the ship. We had been changed, somehow, by our journey, our spirits nourished and our hearts expanded.

Lesson # 7: Life is "Outstanding"

We never stop making excuses for not living our lives full-out. The reasons all seem valid enough — there's not enough money, time, energy, space, whatever! But behind our scenes of action — or inaction— come our mind and the thoughts it generates; it controls our actions.

I had a client once explain to me that being negative was being realistic. He believed that if you think you won't get something, then when you do get it, it will be a pleasant surprise. In this man's opinion, thinking negatively prevented him from disappointment. In fact, it did the exact opposite. His marriage was rocky, his business was not as profitable as it could have been, and his relationship with his kids was strained.

Our thoughts create our reality. Our minds are infinitely more powerful and creative than we can ever imagine. Once we understand that what we think and believe creates reality in some form or another, then we become guardians of our thoughts. I see this played out in the lives of my clients over and over again. When I suggest they behave differently towards something, I often get the response, "this will be hard." Well, if you think it will be hard it definitely *will* be hard and the opportunity to fail will grow.

On the other hand, if you say to yourself, "I am able to do this," or "I am in the process of change," then you create an environment of possibilities.

Once we have positive new thoughts, we need to open our eyes and become very aware of how situations, people and things start manifesting themselves. When people talk about manifesting something, what they're really talking about is the arrival in our lives of the things we want to see there.

It's important to trust that what is showing up in your life is a direct result of what you've been thinking about and how you've given those thoughts life through your own actions and behaviour. (Remember Gamin?) So how do we start all this when we come from a place of fear?

The first step is to set your intentions on a daily basis. Before you get out of bed in the morning, connect with your thoughts and emotions and set your desires for the day. You might simply decide that you desire a peaceful day, or that you intend to meet just the right people for your business; perhaps you might want to affect someone in a positive way, or have the opportunity to do a kindness for someone "just because."

No matter what the intention, the fact that you have programmed your emotional GPS means you are already headed in the right direction. It's a good idea to start with a sense of gratitude for all the blessings and gifts in your life, and for the ones that are coming.

Know with absolute certainty that your life can change in less than one second. All the dreams, hopes and ambitions that you have for the future might end up meaning nothing at all. Have an attitude of gratitude for what exists in your life in this present moment because that is all we have — the present.

The second step is to listen actively, attentively and curiously to the language you use on yourself. Those silent words and sentences that no one hears are very powerful, and they can throw you into a blue mood fast! In the beginning, just focus on becoming aware of your negative "self-talk."

Everything starts with awareness and everything is a lesson. I'll talk a bit more about the power of "The Lesson" later. Much of how we think about things is based in our history, but how our brains function is also important.

Neurons that fire together wire together. Imagine that each thought you think leaves a cookie in your brain — similar to the ones that get deposited on your computer during online browsing. The more you visit a site, the more cookies you leave.

The brain is miraculous because with repeated thoughts, the chain of cookie becomes so strong that it becomes a neural cookie highway. Given this fact then, we need to be gentle and compassionate with ourselves as we rethink old thought patterns and replace them with new thoughts (cookies). It takes time!

We are so used to tuning in and turning on instantly that we expect that thinking one positive thought will change the brain. Not so. It can take many positive thoughts repeated many times in order to make change.

How exciting is that?! You can reprogram your brain by repetition.

The third step in transforming a fear-based set of thought patterns into one that serves us well is to turn your negatives into positives.

Decide that the negative doesn't serve you anymore and that the positive thoughts are much more nourishing. This is similar to making a good food choice:

we know which foods are better for our bodies and so we choose them because we know they are better.

Sometimes we choose the junk, but then we know that our bodies will become junk heaps if we don't control ourselves, right? The mind is the same: negative junk produces a junky brain and because the brain is connecting to absolutely everything inside and around us, it's only a matter of time before the body responds to the junky brain.

North American medicine loves to separate the physical symptoms from everything else. Doctors use a medical model where they treat the symptoms, usually with drugs, and treat them with no conscious knitting-in of our mental and emotional state. This is ridiculous. We know now that all of our physical systems are linked together like a chain. You affect the body by exercise and at the same time the mind becomes clearer and the emotions become lighter.

Negativity produces negative energy just as positivity produces positive energy. Try this experiment. The next time you walk into a room with people in it, feel how the room and the energy may feel negative or positive. The operative word in that last sentence is "feel." We have more nerve endings in our gut than in our spines, yet we constantly intellectualize our gut responses.

Here is another explanation. Our brains have not changed since prehistoric times, and in those days, humankind's gut instincts kept prehistoric people alive.

They still do. How many times have you just missed an accident and known that if you had been at that intersection five seconds earlier, you would have been in the crash?

Some notion or sense told you to slow down or take a breath — something triggered you to do something different.

Our intuitions are similar to radar and we need to respect the power and feel the guidance. Use less brain and more gut.

Life is Outstanding Reflections

Take some time right now and start writing without editing yourself. Allow your thoughts to flow freely as you think of these questions:

What is preventing you from experiencing your best life ever?

If you could change one thing to make your life OUTSTANDING, what would that be?

What is stopping you from doing just that?

What do you feel you are missing in your life?

What is preventing you from providing the missing piece or pieces?

How long are you willing to wait to start consciously creating your life?

Chapter 8 — Walking on the Edge

In honour of my 55th birthday, I decided to conquer my fear of heights so I booked the Edge Walk experience at the CN Tower in Toronto. Basically, you walk on a metal sidewalk around the circumference of the CN Tower, *outside*. You are tethered to a line that holds up to 15,000 pounds, and I guess they tell you this because trusting in the equipment is essential for a positive experience.

But let's backtrack a bit.

While I had been in the process of purchasing this experience online, my husband Doug had walked into the room. He looked at the numbers on the screen and expressed surprise at the cost — he thought it was too much money for the two of us. Well, that's funny, I thought, I hadn't actually thought of inviting him to come along with me! Calmly, I told him I had decided to do this on my own and that I hadn't really thought he would come along with me anyway.

Doug left the room and after a loud silence, he came back in and said "OK, I'll do it too." Doug has no fear of heights, so it was a purely fun adventure for him; when I look at the pre- and post-event excitement the adventure caused, I'd say he definitely got his money's worth!

In the weeks leading up to the walk, we told many people we were going to be doing it, and their reactions alone were worth the price of admission! We were excited but I couldn't help feeling a slight tingle of anxiety as I thought of what I was heading off to do. I was afraid of heights! Wasn't I?

Finally the day arrived. We took the train into Toronto from Burlington and as we approached Union Station, we could see the people at the top of the tower. My stomach started to get nervous and excited, more in anticipation than dread.

We arrived at the check-in, where we had to sign a million documents saying CN was not legally liable if we died! Of course there was a medical form and it asked if either of us had asthma. Doug does have asthma and I panicked (typical reaction), worried that the height would bring on an asthma attack. Maybe we should tell them? But what if we weren't allowed to do the walk as a result? And...my monkey brain continued on and on until Doug looked at me and reminded me that he had flown in many planes! Oh right, good to go then — whew!

Onwards to the waiting room. Staff clustered us in to groups of six and we piled into another room where we received our snazzy overalls, heard about all the safety checks, and listened to a run-down on what was going to happen at the top of the tower. They checked us for absolutely everything: alcohol, drugs, loose clothing, jewelry. Once that was done, they outfitted us in our gear and each guide checked all the buckles, belts and contraptions at least 10 times. Then we waited. Tick

tick tick. And with each second that passed I became increasingly nervous. Fretfully, we all started chatting with each other and it seemed as though everyone was experiencing some sort of heightened emotion. Some were excited, terrified, and anxious, and the lovely outcome was that we were all strangers when we walked in, but we quickly bonded through our emotions. There was a connection of spirit among us and a propping up and support that was quite warming and calming.

It was finally time to take the elevator to the top of the CN Tower. As we left the elevator to stand in the vestibule, we were checked once again for our buckle security and then hooked up to an overhead track. Guess what held the whole thing together at the end? Cable ties! Yup my life was being protected by cable ties. That gave me such a secure feeling!

By this time, I was able to see outside and I temporarily felt paralyzed. I was definitely in flight or fight mode, but just hadn't decided on which path to follow yet. I looked at the others and they seemed nervous but OK, except for my husband. He was truly and authentically excited to step on the edge of the platform.

The guide got Doug to be the leader of our pack and off we went. I had decided to stay and not run away but I did ask the guide how many people decided not to do the walk at the last minute. He told me that out of the 7000 people that have started out, four balked and didn't do it. They were all men! Huh! Super power!

When my turn came to step out onto the edge, my feet froze. It was similar to the feeling I had when I was about to have my first swing on a circus trapeze. There I was, standing at the top of an endless ladder, thinking about marriage and death and how similar they can be, and all my feet and legs could do was hold me there, frozen, and scream, "NO, don't do it!"

However, I was there to conquer my fear of heights and even if it killed me first, I was going to do it. Out I stepped and tippy-toed my way forward. The guide got all of us in a line for the first event which was called "Toes over Toronto." We all had to go to the edge of the walkway and wiggle out so the middles of our feet were on the walk and our toes were over the edge. Then we were instructed to lean into the harness (think girl on deck of the Titanic with arms spread out).

Doug immediately went into it smiling and yelping the whole time and I, on the other hand, screamed the whole time but I did it. I was so scared, but my fear was less about my own feelings and more about Doug. He was so free and flowing that he was walking around and in and out and leaning over, so I kept screaming at him to "get back" — oh my, when did I become his mother?

Off to the next event. We walked another bit along the walkway and we saw a plane coming in to land at the Toronto Island Airport. I had never seen a plane that close, mind you! It was thrilling! For our next trick we had to walk backwards up to the edge keeping our toes on the platform and our heels over the edge. Then we had to lean backwards (think backwards Titanic girl). That's when I didn't think I would make it. The guide was great; he kept encouraging me to take one more baby step until I reached the edge (not looking down for one moment). My husband just leaned back and spread his arms out with this delightful smile on his face that said "heaven." I, on the other hand, felt paralyzed, yet oddly curious. My legs felt rubbery so I had to sit in my harness and then straighten my legs to a standing position. As soon as the guide was ready to go to the next station, I gratefully and quickly walked back to the middle of the sidewalk.

The next stop on our tour involved a bit of tourist attraction info: the million-dollar condo, Toronto Island, the airport. It was all quite pleasant because we weren't moving. I started to become aware that I was calming down and actually enjoying the experience.

The twenty minutes was up and it was time to get off the edge and back on the ground. Despite the initial terror, I know I could have walked around again and really enjoyed the experience.

Lesson #8: Live Where You Fear to Live-Rumi

Irrational fears are the unfounded fears that strike at the very heart our existence. When we are able to feel the fear generated by some past event, we can work through that fear in many ways by desensitizing our memory and laying down new mental tracks. Neurons that fire together wire together so we can reprogram our brains to match a better memory to a past event.

When we just fear something instinctively, it is tougher to blast through it to a place of acceptance and peace. It has been my experience that the fear that holds us the most points the way to the exact thing we need to do to liberate ourselves from its hold.

Thinking about it doesn't work. It's the doing that shows us the fear is nothing but imagination gone wonky. I have also noticed that when people see the picture of me on the walk they say one of three things: "Wow! That looks awesome," "You must be crazy," or "I could never do that!"

It's the last thought that I am going to explore. **I could never do that!** When we think like this, what are the odds that we will never do "that?" The answer: 100%. What if we took the words we use to describe the event and instead say, "That looks like an enriching experience"? Viewed from this framework, we open ourselves to the possibility that this action, or any action or event, has the potential to nourish — and that potential leads to growth.

I was once a witness in a divorce trial. The father was suing for custody of his two sons and since I was the only therapist to have provided marital counselling, my testimony was critical to the outcome of the case. When I met with the lawyer and he told me I was going to be called to court, I went immediately into panic mode. We therapists dread this day because there is always a concern that sufficient notes were taken to argue the case without bias. Not only that, but being in a courtroom can be very intimidating. You are sitting in a small area in front of two lawyers, one of whom needs to discredit you, pick everything that you say apart, and basically plant enough doubt about your testimony that it won't affect the outcome of the case. Beside you sits the judge, who is listening intently to every word you say and who is also taking notes.

With all that in mind, the lawyer smiled gently at me and said "Heidi, just look at it as an enriching experience." I laughed out loud. "Who are you kidding? Enriching!" He continued to smile and calmly explained that this was the only way to get through the experience. So I took his advice.

The day came and all the witnesses gathered together in the outer room of the courtroom and waited to be called to the witness stand. That was interesting all on its own because we were told by the judge that there was to be absolutely no discussion of the case and believe me, we were all dying to talk about it.

As each person was called in, the others left behind took deep breaths, knowing their time was coming soon. Then, when the previous witness left the courtroom and came back into the waiting area, the look on their face said it all. This was not an enriching experience at all! Just as I had thought — that lawyer was a rascal for even suggesting the idea!

Finally it was my turn. I was so nervous I thought my heart was beating in my throat instead of in my chest. I kept repeating "enriching, enriching, enriching," and then I saw the two lawyers in their long black robes. They looked so fierce and combative, but I kept repeating, "enriching."

Then a strange thing happened. My body actually calmed down and released the panic. I felt as if I had become an observer, detached from the personal feeling of being raked over the coals. I looked at the lawyers as men playing a game of strategy not men wishing to destroy my reputation. I felt calm and focused and answered their questions with confidence and clarity.

So what happened there? Initially, the fear of testifying had actually triggered my deeper feelings of lack of self-worth. Out came the quiet self-deprecating conversation that says "I am not good enough, I didn't take enough notes, I am terrible at my career, I don't have enough qualifications," etc. In that context, the fear felt real because it triggered a negative response.

When I was able to personally detach from the experience, my trigger stopped firing and the "true" me was able to shine. One of my teachers advised me that when we remove doubt and personal attachment to a situation, we experience the freedom to create the true outcome.

Fear can also be about protection. Our intuition often tells us to avoid certain people or circumstances because our higher self is protecting our emotional, psychological or physical health. This fear response feels different energetically from the fear that is irrational or sprouting from self limiting beliefs. This protective fear response feels like a "knowing," and it is usually located in the heart or stomach area. The "knowing" feels comfortable and right but because we tend to intellectualize things, we go from a comfortable knowing to an uncomfortable position of doubt. It is at this point that we make mistakes in our judgment.

Live Where You Fear to Live Reflections

Take some time right now and start writing without editing yourself. Allow your thoughts to flow freely as you think of these questions:

How does fear stop you from living?

Are you aware of how fear is a reflection of negative thought patterns?

Why do you fear change?

What stops you from pushing yourself to the edge of thought or experience?

Think of times when you have been afraid. What were the outcomes?

Lesson #9: Moving Forward: Bringing It All Together

I love the word "genesis" because to me it describes the beginning of everything, and absolutely everything *is* a beginning. As you take a breath in, it's the beginning of a new breath, constantly renewing and rejuvenating and keeping you alive from the beginning of one moment and breath to the beginning of another moment and breath. It's like floating on an air mattress as the gentle waves quietly lift you from one wave to another, always to the beginning of the next wave.

I thought to put this chapter about beginnings at the start of the book until I realized that all my experiences led me to this place of moving forward. My experiences created the desire and the need to have a fluid, dynamic, musical, and hopeful presence and life.

Do I still get trapped in negative thought patterns? Of course — but they are only brief and I am aware of them. The awareness is a key factor. Once we are aware of the limiting beliefs, the negativity language and the self-judgment, then we can choose to either sit with it or change it.

The fact that awareness produces choice is the fundamental principal to operating from a place of wholeness versus a place of insecurity and doubt. Whether we choose to change our thoughts or not doesn't matter, it's the genesis of awareness that matters. I think choice is one of the basic freedoms that was given to us at birth and, as we mature, we place fences around ourselves that prevent us from thinking that we **can** make a choice. Those fences can be anything — our expectations, what we perceive society expects from us, what we think our roles are, our fear of what other people will think or say, or our insecurities, fears, and doubts.

I know what it feels like to be stuck and how liberating it feels to move forward. Around January of last year, I hit a major roadblock in my life. I had come to feel as if I had failed at being an entrepreneur. I was in debt more than I wanted to be, I had made some decisions that were not in my best interests and the dream I had to establish a new and creative business model had just not come to fruition.

I started to feel very sorry for myself and created a case that basically said, "go get a real job!" So I closed down my office in Burlington and went away for a two-week vacation in Italy.

Upon my return, I shared office space with a friend of mine three days a week while actively looking for a job. Funny thing about the universe — it always gives you what you are attracting and I was attracting and manifesting scarcity.

The phone stopped ringing and people were not coming to my new location. Some of my older clients asked me to meet them at coffee shops in Burlington so I found myself driving to the office and then driving back through Burlington to meet people at the coffee shops. Thankfully, one day I ended up visiting a friend who owned an amazing business called "The Think Spot." I found myself standing in the kitchen and for the first time in a long time, I felt safe. That feeling was so positively overwhelming that I can still experience it very profoundly today. My friend offered me some office space at no charge and I jumped at the opportunity. Sure enough, the phone started to ring off the hook.

Sometime later, I was finishing up with a client I hadn't seen in two years and as he stood up to say goodbye, he looked at me and said "Heidi, you are a beautiful person." This was another profound, life-altering moment.

I realized right then that there was not a company around that would tell me that I was a beautiful person. Not only that, but with his comment he made me understand that I have and can continue to make a real difference in the lives of many people.

At that point, I questioned everything. I still knew that I needed a different direction, but just not the direction I had thought I needed.

As I write this, living my life with purpose and passion and knowing what I know today, I understand that the events of my life were all meant to happen, and in fact they *had to* happen. What's more, they all unfolded according to divine timing and order to create where I am today and where I am going tomorrow.

Everything that has happened to me has been a beginning and has represented the ongoing genesis of the new life I've been creating, the new me I have been uncovering.

It has happened like magic. From touching whales to testifying in court, my life has taken me on a sparkling journey, although I have not always appreciated it as such. But by being open to the adventure, I've been able to let go of many of the fears and beliefs that had kept me from living a full and happy life, and I've been able to embrace a set of perspectives that have helped my heart learn to fly.

I want that for you too! As you make your own tentative and hopeful trek to a compelling and rewarding future of your own, know that I'm cheering you on from the sidelines. Your path might seem difficult and littered with problems. You might not be sure where it's leading you. But *it's possible* for you to find your way to the clearing space of life, that place where possibilities become realities.

Just take it one step at a time.

And never give up on yourself.

You are worth the journey.

About the Author

Heidi Cowie, motivational Speaker, radio show host – and now author of the remarkable breakthrough book *Touch the Whale*.

Cowie has celebrated ten years of being in private practice as a therapist. She has coached, educated, inspired, and counselled thousands of people to move from a state of struggle to state of peace, acceptance, and hope. Skillfully combining her corporate experience of 25 years with good old-fashioned common sense, Heidi is an expert in counselling her client in the many issues they face.

She also shares her information freely with an eye to helping the general population recognize the effects of stress. She has been quoted as a relationship expert in The Hamilton Spectator, The Toronto Sun, Readers Digest, Parenting Magazine, CH Television and Rogers Daytime.

Cowie's past published books include *Overgivers - Walking the Tightrope Between Love and Guilt*.

Cowie is also a motivational speaker and has given presentations to well over 3,000 people. Every Friday she hosts her own radio station show, Heidi Radio, where she interviews exciting and motivational guest who are living their lives on purpose and with passion.

Touch the Whale

Manor House
905-648-2193
www.manor-house.biz

www.ingramcontent.com/pod-product-compliance
Lightning Source LLC
Chambersburg PA
CBHW021119080526
44587CB00010B/574